PERSONAL DEVELOPMENT

THE 76 UNBREAKABLE LAWS FOR YOUR PERSONAL DEVELOPMENT

INDEX

PERSONAL DEVELOPMENT

BOOK 1

PERSONAL DEVELOPMENT

Foreword

This book will help you make smart decisions on your personal development journey and follow through courageously. This means having the maturity to take one hundred percent responsibility for your well-being, your vocation, your money resources, your relationships, your emotions, your habits, and your spiritual notions.

It requires you to look deeply into yourself, to consciously choose what kind of individual you really are on the inside, and then to bring your outer reality into congruence with your inner self. The goal is to help you achieve outstanding effectiveness while maintaining inner balance, where your notions, feelings, actions and abilities are working collectively to produce the life you really want.

These personal development issues will serve as a great start if you are beginning to develop yourself.

They will put you on the right track to control any situation, achieve goals and become a better individual.

Chapter 1: Healthy Abundant Mind

Don't live in the scarcity mentality

This is the psychological state where thoughts of rivalry originate. If you know there isn't enough to go around, you'll try to rush in and take something from someone else.

There is enough.

It may be difficult for you to think that rivalry is wrong since it is so valued in our society. It feels as if every politician or other well-paid employee thinks that only competition gets what is needed.

But that is why they are employees. They do not realize that by not participating in the competition they would become independent and free, even as their natural state should be.

When they recognize that competition is wrong and stop trying to gain something at the expense of other people, they gradually fall into the mentality of abundance. You begin to recognize that you are capable of getting everything you think, and this assures you that there will constantly be more than enough of everything for everyone.

However, what if you still have the mentality of scarcity and do not know how to get out of it? You will need to introduce a positive affirmation into your daily life. It may sound like this: I see abundance everywhere.

Or it can be put this way: There are more than enough resources in the world for everyone. Whatever appeals to you the most.

In the same way you will have to train your eyes not to see what you don't want to see in your life. If you wish to eliminate thoughts of scarcity, turn your attention to the manifestations of abundance. Look at the lush nature, the fancy cars, the singing morning birds, the positive and rich individuals, the real buildings, everything you affiliate with abundance.

There are many symbols of wealth to choose from, it simply depends on what symbols constitute wealth for you. I can see nature and see proof of pure abundance on this Earth; however, other people can see the symbols of abundance by seeing new gadgets and fancy clothes.

When you train your eyes to focus on such symbols, you will begin the process that originated in you. Your thinking will change absolutely as you no longer see the manifestations of poverty. By always looking at the symbols of wealth, you will develop the desire to be abundant.

As you now focus easily on abundance, you will have no difficulty in producing thoughts of abundance. These thoughts will manifest in your life bringing all that you have thought deeply.

An abundance mentality tells you that there are constantly new opportunities and possibilities. This releases much of the pressure you might feel if you have a scarcity mindset that makes you believe you only have this one opportunity at this time. Or it makes you feel like a perfect failure simply because you've made a mistake and things haven't worked out.

A mindset of abundance allows you to see life in a more long-term perspective. And it can help you perform better because you are producing far less pressure and anxiety within your own brain.

If you have a scarcity mentality, you probably take things too seriously. You may think to yourself, "If I fail, the sky will fall. However, you probably won't. But if you think you do, you become overly nervous and have produced a self-fulfilling prophecy of failure, as your self-created inner negativity puts obstacles in your path to success.

Chapter 2: Meditation

Meditation lays a great foundation for success. It prepares the mental soil for the seeds of abundance (if you so choose).

Meditation eliminates negative thinking and gets rid of harmful emotions in your head. I'm not exactly sure why that happens, but it may be because with the practice of meditation you enter a lower frequency of brain activity. In that state the cleansing process can occur.

The power within

You will not eliminate all negative thoughts after meditating once, however, with continuous meditation you will progress to such a state.

You will notice that after meditation you will feel at peace.

There are not many thoughts circulating in your brain and you feel harmony within. I can describe this feeling as having been protected from adverse thoughts, events and other harmful occurrences.

You feel calm and good.

Occasionally you will go into deep meditation (theta state). You will become so disengaged from your brain that you will align yourself with the universe and that will make you have a lot of incredible ideas.

That occurs to me very often since I've been meditating for a while. The amazing ideas just flow into you and you get those 'wow'... moments when you can't believe that you ever noticed such amazing thinking.

In the same way I get reminders with meditation of what I need to do to achieve a certain goal. It is as if the consciousness recognizes precisely what I must do and constantly reminds me of things I would otherwise forget.

As soon as you begin to implement this notion of personal development, you will feel less stressed and eventually not stressed at all. Harmful events will not affect you as much because you will care less. Your main focus will be on matters that are big and valuable.

You will begin to feel joy for no apparent reason. You will catch yourself in the moments of perfect peace and happiness. It will seem that there is nothing wrong with this creation and that you are the happiest individual in the world. This is a magical state produced by meditation. Such a state should be a natural state for everyone, but for most individuals this state is out of the question to enter because of all the negativity in their minds.

With the additional practice of meditation, your intuition will rise.

You will acquire stronger feelings from within by warning yourself or encouraging you to take action. You should never ignore these signs, as they will only help you to achieve more and become a better individual.

You will understand which foods are good for you and which are bad for you. Naturally, this will not come right away. It may take some time, about two to six months of meditation for some. You could stop eating meat and other foods. That's because your body is telling you that you have been contaminating yourself with food that you don't need.

The most crucial change you will go through is clear thinking.

Because you don't have as many harmful thoughts in your brain, you will begin to see a clear picture of any situation. You will understand exactly what to do and how to proceed in any situation.

Chapter 3: Establishing objectives

Defined goals serve an important purpose. They keep you proactive. Without goals, you respond to conditions and events. Outside things control you. With goals, you produce your own conditions and events. Therefore, you become a master of your destiny.

By adjusting goals, you continue to move forward and improve your life. You can only reach your destination if you specify it. Setting goals is the procedure for doing so. You will not get stuck if you continue to work with this notion of personal development.

Get a plan

The arrangement of the objectives allows you to achieve more comfort in life. The main mistake individuals make is that they set goals for themselves to achieve happiness.

Happiness cannot be the object of your goal. Happiness is something you have inside you all the time. You may not have reached it yet, but it is there.

These general suggestions are organized in a sequence that will help you move from considering your goals to actually achieving them. Don't forget that these are just tips; take what you like and try it out for a while to see what works best for you.

Use a journal to keep a record of your journey toward your goals where you can keep daily or weekly records of your progress, including affirmations, winners, appreciations for your hard work, honors, resistance, obstacles, etc. Use your goal journal to write down your goals first and to rewrite them over time. Use it to break down your goals into steps.

Criticize your progress on a regular basis and take some notes.

It is very important that you put yourself in an inspiring, positive and relaxed state before you write down your goals. Some ideas for getting into a positive state include

Meditation, listening to inspiring music, reading something funny or amusing, watching a funny movie, taking a walk in a beautiful place, exercising or praying.

After entering a great mental and emotional state, begin your brainstorming. Write down all likely goals quickly without editing or criticizing. You can review and prioritize later; at this point you need to be as original as possible.

Here are a number of likely areas of your life that you should consider when developing your goal list: work, finances, relationships, loved ones, home, friends, personal development, well-being, appearance, possessions, fun and recreation, travel, spiritual, self-esteem and service/community.

Goals fall under variable time periods such as: Immediate goals, 30 daily goals, 6-month goals, 1-year goals, 5 years, 10 or more years of vision. Make sure you can achieve what you want in the time frame you have agreed upon.

When you write your goal, say it as if it has already happened. Put your goals in words that assume you have already achieved them. For example, "I now have a new car.

To make you passionate, invested and motivated, add emotional language to your compound goals. Here's an illustration "I absolutely love and am energized about my beautiful new house in the hills" which is much more exciting than "I like my new house.

As your subconscious literally manifests things, you need to set specific and detailed goals. Use language that is clear in describing exactly what you want

Compose on favourable rather than negative terms.

Check with yourself to make sure you are considering what you really want. We often try to please others at our expense. You will not succeed in trying to achieve the goals that your parents, spouse or other acquaintances or relatives want for you.

Think about your most crucial values and

beliefs when developing your goals. For example, if you value freedom, your goal may be to be self-employed. If what you value is safety, you may want to work for the government where layoffs rarely occur.

Choose goals that you can actually achieve in a reasonable amount of time. After brainstorming, one way to prioritize is to put the highest priority goals on ten of the ten possible points and the least crucial on one of the ten.

Break each goal into manageable blocks that produce a step-by-step plan for achieving it. For example, if you need a new car, first decide precisely what color, model, year and make you need. Write this down in your goal journal. Then write down the particular steps you need to take to reach your goal.

Chapter 4: Focus

Focus on the right things. You must pay full attention to the things that will lead you to success. Therefore, instead of spending time doing things that eliminate your chances of success (like watching TV), you should focus on taking actions that will get you there faster.

You should always strive to be proactive and make things happen.

Being reactive causes you to lose focus while you are busy responding to events and conditions that come your way.

You should try not to get caught up in too much. I would suggest eliminating the insignificant ones and focusing on those tasks that benefit you most. You may need to study the 80/20 rule to better understand how to achieve this.

Staying focused can be very difficult.

This leads to the question of how to stay focused on the results we would like to achieve, and keep the brain on target.

Stay focused

Exercise your self-control! It is the hardest thing in the world to stay centered, but you must force your thoughts to stop straying and get back to your point.

Find a purpose that helps you to direct yourself. We often lack motivation or a purpose. Have you ever believed that a purpose is like a push, simply like fuel for a car? Without a big enough reason, you will hardly make it. If the purpose is big enough, then the how always drives itself. Failure is not even a condition.

Clarify your goal. Is it the million dollars you have in mind or is it the boat you can buy if you achieve the goal? Work toward your stated reason in incremental steps - boat today, a million dollars tomorrow.

Repeat a "focus mantra". What you consider is what you have established, even as explained in the Law of Attraction. Your brain gets warmly absorbed by the boat. You read about it, daydream about it, look in the newspapers and travel to boat shops, and slowly but surely produce enough thought energy in that penetrating thought to materialize all the things, individuals, opportunities and cash essential to bringing the boat into your life.

Along the way, you didn't dream of having a million dollars, you dreamed of the boat as your first focused goal. The notion of the boat becomes real to you in an emotionally charged way that the million dollars does not yet have.

Make sure your desire for the purpose is strong enough. The most crucial question you must ask yourself before you attempt to achieve any goal is, do you truly have a strong desire to achieve it, a powerful purpose that drives you, that magical gleam in your eye when you consider it, the certainty of achieving it? If not, the work will be useless. Just look deeper and keep looking for what really drives you.

Don't be afraid to dream a big dream. To keep your brain focused you need big, bold goals. The bigger your purpose, the less trouble you will have in achieving what you have in mind.

Take a break now and then. This helps you to stay focused and refresh your mind. It is recommended that you take a 5 minute break every half hour of work.

Know where you want to be and how long this will take? One should have ideal short, medium and long term goals in the back of the brain. Short-term goals can be a matter of a couple of months or more. Strive to achieve and do your best within a required time frame. This helps reduce complacency and also avoids procrastination.

Constantly remember that procrastination is the thief of time. Stay away from putting off any of your actions by procrastinating for tomorrow, next week, next month and so on. Instead, do them today and move on to the next project.

Chapter 5: Overcome your fear

Fearful individuals never succeed. Their fear prevents them from succeeding and becoming what they want to be. Fear constantly stops progress and stops individuals.

The fastest way to realize this idea of personal development is by confronting fear. However, the simplest way to eliminate fear is to understand that you are in control of everything.

You always manifest your main state of

mind. The world you see around you is the expression of how you feel inside. When you understand this you will fear nothing as you will know that you are capable of producing everything you desire by altering your state of mind.

Be Real

To overcome your fear and make it trivial, you have to make it smaller or make your dreams bigger.

When I started making a living on my own, I had no idea what I was doing, and I was dealing with my own mental ghosts for the first time.

It's only in retrospect that I can see what put me through all this.

Although I didn't know exactly what to do, it was my strength of spirit that kept me going. I was besieged by my own fear; however, I knew what I wanted, so I continued.

Remember, you are in charge of your brain and what goes on inside it.

Take a deep look at your ideas and see how you are seeing what you want and don't want.

You can see them, hear them, or feel them, no matter which. The crucial thing is that you learn to expand what you want and reduce what you don't want.

I'm not talking about putting aside the bad things in your brain, just making them insignificant for now; you can always reverse the procedure later if you want to.

Anything you feel can be altered. What you feel can be altered.

You are in complete control. The only problem is that most individuals are unwilling to claim their power and take responsibility.

Acceptance

The first time I was asked to do an audio interview. I was anxious, yet I knew that to achieve my goal was inevitable. I had to do it eventually. Thinking this way reassured me and encouraged me to do the interview.

I was considering what I wanted. It doesn't matter if you're considering making a living doing what you love or just wishing you had a blog in demand, what makes you tick is great.

This is one of the main ways I defeat my own fears day in and day out. I admit they're there. I look at where I want to go, and I keep going, without thinking much, as if I already know where I have to go, there is no reason to guess, and that will just keep me going.

It works for me. No matter how scared I am, if I'm always honest with myself. I know where I want to go, and I know what I need to do to get there. Any fear is trivial if it holds me back. It's a waste of time.

Everyone deals with fear, but successful individuals take action and are willing to deal with failure and anything else that is dirty.

The only drawback to my procedure is that it doesn't work on issues I'm not passionate about. For example, I'm a little disgusted with insects, spiders, and the like, but I have no motivation to eliminate that fear, since it's not relevant to me.

How to Make Your Fears Trivial

By now, I'm sure you know how you can overcome your fears and turn them into something trivial, but there's still room to make it easier.

If a fear arises, consider where you want to go and if you are moving in the right direction. If you resolve that you are moving in the right direction, acknowledge the fear and keep moving forward.

This procedure requires courage to begin with, but when you are comfortable with it, it becomes easier to believe that it works.

Why is it that when you walk down the street and come across a sign that says "construction, do not enter", you directly consider the best way to avoid it and keep moving forward, but when you are heading for a more fulfilling life and something gets in your way, you stay dead?

It is because of your discipline, programming and the affiliations you have made in your life.

Everything can change. Remember, you have the ability to do whatever you want. There are no excuses.

Every time I face one of my fears, it fades and eventually disappears. The hardest part is doing it the first few times.

To get the courage to move forward, I look at the options of bending over my fear and moving through it. Life almost always seems bigger when you face your fears.

If I buckle down to my fear, I will live a life of sadness. If I face my fear, I will continue to grow and move toward a fuller life.

You have to find a way to incite yourself. Start by taking action and learning how your brain works. It's simple to believe that your brain, your thoughts and your feelings are in charge, but if that's real, why are you able to observe your thoughts and feelings when you're fully present?

How can your thoughts be in control if there is a supervisor watching them? They can't. Breathe, relax, and be in the now, and you become the observer.

Chapter 6: Thanks

Gratitude brings you more and more things you are grateful for. This is because the cosmos reacts to your gratitude by giving you more than you are grateful for.

Being grateful is the reason, getting more of what you are grateful for is the effect. Every action has a particular reaction; therefore, gratitude has this particular reaction that may never change.

Gratitude is a really powerful force that reaches the object you are thankful for immediately. In the same way it brings you to a harmonious state in alignment with the cosmos. This puts you in a flow of life that makes you develop success effortlessly.

Be grateful for

Among the best things you can do is to be grateful; for everything you have, for everything you have done, for all the individuals in your life, and for the developmental procedure. It's crucial. Gratitude is one of the highest vibrations in this life, and it attracts a surplus in your life.

Without gratitude one can become arrogant and isolated. Until you truly look at all that you have, and treasure all that you have been given, things may not make sense. Did you have something to do with your appearance? Or the color of your eyes? Or a completely healthy body? Or the place where you were born? No, not at all.

Be grateful for everything that has been produced for you. Think that you are able to see clearly the trees and the beauty around you, that you are able to take a breath of fresh air, that today and right where you are, you are capable of so many things. Be grateful for the knowledge that has been presented to you or that you have learned.

Be thankful that you have so many individuals who love you deeply. Be thankful for every experience that has strengthened and shaped you as the individual you will become. It is easy to say "I did all this," but there are so many individuals who have contributed both knowingly and unknowingly to your success, your emotional support, the balance in your life, and your power. There is a force in your life right now that keeps you on track; be aware of it.

There are individuals you know who have a profound effect on you in a meeting. There are others with whom you formulate relationships over time. There are instructors who are great, but you don't really know their effect until many years later. There are guides who have fortunately been placed on your path at the right time, to comfort or fortify you. There are several who respect you simply for who you are, what you claim, and how you have touched your life. Be grateful for all of this.

In a spirit of gratitude, you will be able to call things to you before they have unfolded. That gratitude declares to the universe that you are open to receive and that you have already received something in your heart.

You put into action a reason and an effect that the universe produces according to your encouragement and gratitude.

Gratitude attracts you like a magnet. When you wish to produce and receive, thank the cosmos for bringing it to you before it happens and it will manifest for you. "Thank you for healing me." "Thank you for bringing the right person to me. "Thank you for my house with the big windows.

Put it away with gratitude and stay open for him and he's on his way. It may take some time as only the right set of conditions need to be met to provide you with the best results.

Oh, and one thing about gratitude, you have to feel it. You can't just pretend. When you have gratitude there is a shift of power to a higher vibration in your body that interacts with the universal power.

Without that shift of energy modification, you will not manifest the way you wish. Without gratitude there is likely to be a stagnation of anything new that can come to you. And occasionally you experience an inversion, as if you are not grateful for what you have, it begins to go away.

Practice gratitude today. Don't take anything for granted. This moment is so brief. Make a list of 10 things right now that you're grateful for.

Say it or read it out loud daily. It only takes a few minutes to alter your thinking, and therefore your reception.

Chapter 7: Display

This idea of personal development will keep you moving forward in life and present you with clues and opportunities to achieve what you are envisioning.

If you keep an image in mind for a while without being distracted, you will make that image manifest.

After the visualization you can begin to see clues about what you need to do to achieve your desires. Be sure to act on them to bring your visualization to the truth.

Be aware that this idea of personal development does not work alone. If your constant psychological state is negative, 10 minutes a day of visualization will not bring you success.

This is because when you visualize your desires, your negative state of mind serves as an obstacle that prevents you from acquiring what you desire.

What you visualized has already manifested in the intangible world, however, the manifestations are prevented from reaching you because of your mind.

Therefore, if you are still negative, you must first work on your state of mind. Once your brain becomes neutral or positive, the visualization will act as the acceleration of the manifestation of your goals.

See

Write down everything you've ever wanted. Go ahead, have fun! There are no limits here. Suppose you have a fairy godmother who can grant you any wish you want and you are able to have everything you have ever wanted.

Do you think that's impossible? Don't think it! Just write down what comes to mind that you want, things, individuals and places you want to go, things you want to do, individuals you want to meet, your dreams and so on. Write down at least fifty things you always wanted.

This is the part you have to work on the most. However, did I mention that it's fun? Do you have that list of things you've always wanted?

Read the list of things you wished for, consider them, and then prioritize them.

Then buy a board, it can be a sticky board or a cork board or even just cardboard. Actually, you just need a board on which you can stick photos. Take out your magazines and scissors and start cutting out photos that you can relate to your wish list.

Once you have enough photos, glue those photos to the board you've prepared. Voilà!

Your vision board is ready!

Now look at your vision board a lot and really look at yourself in the situations you want to provoke. Remember to keep a positive mindset.

Conclusion

Discipline is really crucial to the self-improvement procedure. Your whole life will be much bigger if you conquer yourself.

When you master self-control, you will become a totally different individual. You will understand much more than you had understood before. You will be able to set goals and actually achieve them, your fears will be gone and a whole new life will be ahead of you.

How to do it? First of all you need to understand that you are not your emotions. You are not your thought. You are not your ego. You are part of the total consciousness. Thought, self-control and emotions were given to you as tools to use in this life. You are none of these things.

When you understand this and control all your aspects, you will conquer yourself. You will become totally disciplined and be able to achieve whatever you want.

Individuals commonly desire quick results, but when they realize what it takes to achieve them, they become discouraged by the whole process of self-improvement. If you feel this way, try to recognize the incredible benefits you will get when you take big steps in your personal development.

Now it's your turn to choose if you still want to accelerate your personal development. This is a really exciting path, but it requires work on your part.

THE 76 UNBREAKABLE LAWS FOR YOUR PERSONAL DEVELOPMENT

BOOK 2

THE 76 UNBREAKABLE LAWS FOR YOUR PERSONAL DEVELOPMENT

- ## <u>LAW 1 : Just do it</u>

The first step is always the hardest. Your mind will create all sorts of scenarios to prevent you from taking that terrifying first step toward your goal.

But that doesn't mean you're a coward. It's just the way your brain defends itself.

Sometimes you have to listen to what your heart has to say and just do it. Everything else will be much easier once you overcome the first obstacle and it is to ignore your brain's terrible warnings and follow your instinct. It's just about making that leap of faith.

- **<u>LAW 2: Doing something does not always imply that it is physical.</u>**

Don't confuse the need to take action with the need to do something literally or physically. There are many other ways to take action without even lifting a finger. For that matter, consider the act of planning.

It is never wise to try to reach a goal without a plan. It is very important that you make a step-by-step plan to achieve it. A good plan takes into account all the potential consequences, as well as all the possible paths you can take to reach your goal.

• <u>LAW 3: Breathing</u>

It is normal to feel uncomfortable when you leave your comfort zone to reach your goal. Acting is often synonymous with taking risks.

You are nervous because you know that risks can end in success or failure, and who wants to end in failure?

Whenever you feel that a situation is overcoming you, take a deep breath. Better yet, take several deep breaths. Studies show how breathing can effectively clear the mind and help calm nerves.

- **<u>LAW 4: Read the biographies of people who achieved their success and that you see yourself reflected in them.</u>**

You may think that you are the only one who is suffering a certain kind of problem of some magnitude in this world, but you are not. With a little research, you will surely find something in common with ordinary and extraordinary people.

Think that we all have a brain and the only thing that can differentiate it from the person who achieved that success is in the mind. So when in doubt, read biographies of people who feel identified, and who are people who have achieved the success you want and who motivate you to keep going. Try to find the small but essential similarities with that individual.

- # LAW 5 : Take small steps

Don't strive to accomplish the same things with the same amount of time and resources as other people. In the end, you have to remind yourself that each person is unique and, consequently, his or her own set of strengths and weaknesses.

In addition, it may be that you are just starting out and that the other person you are comparing with is years ahead of you in terms of skill and experience. The other person can't afford to take baby steps, but you can and should. If you rush things too fast, everything can end up like you didn't plan it in your mind.

- ## <u>LAW 6: Nothing is built in a day</u>

It's good to have a plan for everything, but you don't have to do everything in one day. Even if you have the energy to do it, the people around you who also have something at stake to achieve your shared goals may not have the time and similar energy to do it. Give them a break. If you have all worked really hard, then you all deserve to rest. There is always a tomorrow to think about.

- ## <u>LAW 7: Don't push yourself</u>

Pressing oneself is different from motivating oneself. Motivating yourself will cause you to take action while pressuring yourself will only succeed in freezing your limbs and brain cells in a state of inaction. Remember that motivation is linked to everything positive, while pressures, and especially excessive ones, to the negative.

- ## **<u>LAW 8: A little competition is good, but don't overdo it.</u>**

Competition can cause you to act because the longer you delay, the longer you will delay in achieving your goal. Friendly competition is also effective in keeping you focused and excited, but be careful. If you let yourself concentrate too much on the competition, you may end up forgetting the general situation. In the end, being too competitive can be another source of distraction that you don't need at all.

- ## **<u>LAW 9: Believe in yourself</u>**

Taking action requires you to have faith in yourself, especially when everyone around you tells you that you can't do it. In the end, you have to remember that you know yourself better than anyone else. You know what you are capable of, and if you believe that the goal you have in mind is within your reach, then it really is, no matter what others say. Go for it.

• <u>LAW 10: Get a partner</u>

Just because you have someone with you and who is willing to help you doesn't mean you haven't been strong enough to achieve your goal. It also doesn't make your goal less satisfying. When you are accompanied on a project, the goal becomes sweeter because you have someone to share it with, you can even consider that partner, a guide that you will both nurture together.

Keep in mind that when you are going to start a project with another person, before doing so prioritize that both have the same goals and similar mentalities. That is why, before starting, have a communication about what each one thinks and feels and what visions they have, since it is a fundamental requirement when you are going to have a partnership with someone.

- ## **<u>LAW 11: Get someone to do it for you</u>**

Taking action also doesn't mean you have to do everything alone. Say that your goal is to build a house. Does that mean you have to do everything from putting up boards to painting walls? Of course not.

Taking action can also mean finding the best person to do the job. So don't be shy about admitting if something is beyond your real knowledge, skills and abilities. There are some things in life that are best left in the hands of an expert. That's why it's very important that you know how to delegate.

• <u>LAW 12: Don't be too proud to ask for help</u>

Many people confuse taking action with doing something that directly contributes to achieving a particular goal. What they don't understand is that sometimes indirect benefits are also important.

Consider, for example, the act of forgetting your pride. Some people may say it has nothing to do with achieving a certain kind of goal, but what if it's your pride that keeps you from getting much-needed expert help?

• <u>LAW 13 : It's okay to start over</u>

What if there comes a time when he realizes that the first step he took was the wrong one? Or what if he suddenly realizes that what he is doing does not lead him toward his goal, but, on the contrary, takes him away from it? Do you sit and cry? If so, it is not the same as taking action. You may be doing something, but it is nothing that can help you achieve your goal.

If you realize that something is wrong, then clear your mind and retrace your steps until you discover that critical mistake you made. Correct it and move on. If you have to, start from scratch, and the sooner, the better.

- ## <u>LAW 14: Never stop trying!</u>

As mentioned earlier, the process of reaching one's goal never ends.

Taking action also means you have to get back on your feet if you trip or fall. It's even okay if you have to start all over again. In the end, what is critical is that you don't let your failures prevent you from taking action and moving forward continuously.

So go ahead, get up and learn from your mistakes. You will be a better and stronger person to do this.

- ## <u>LAW 15: Have a backup plan</u>

Plans, like rules, are meant to be broken. And you need to be prepared for that eventuality from the beginning, having a contingency or backup plan in place.

Others think backup plans are similar to admitting failure. It's not. Rather, backup plans are really just a way of recognizing the fact that change is the only thing that is constant in the world. There is no way to predict what will happen next minute, but you can try to prepare for things that might happen. Think of it as a way to soften the way you take action to achieve your goal.

- ## <u>LAW 16 : Consider your resources</u>

Taking action will give you the direction, but that's not what this is about. You also need to consider the resources you have at hand. How do you make the most of it? What other resources do you need to make a move? Where can you get them?

Will power and motivation, as well as concentration, are great things to keep in mind, but these are internal resources. You also need to back up your plan with specific external resources such as money, labor, and skills, among other things to keep in mind.

- ## **<u>LAW 17 : Look before you jump, but jump anyway if you have to.</u>**

There are two types of risks: manageable and unmanageable. You are lucky if all the things you have to do to reach your goal involve manageable risks. But what if it's not? Should you back off and let all your previous hard work go to waste?

Risks are scary, and it's a good thing you're aware of that. Those who think they can take any kind of risk are simply reckless and reckless. They are certainly not brave or exceptionally intelligent.

If you come across an unmanageable risk or one where the stakes are too high, look before you jump. Consider the ups and downs, but the most important thing of all is that you consider what your brain and guts have to say. Then jump but always do it with Faith.

- ## **LAW 18: Don't be too rigid or stubborn**

He's got to know when to change tactics. Your plan may seem fantastic and absolutely brilliant, but many things in the real world are unpredictable and can spoil your tactics.

You have to be aware of when to stop hitting the wall and find another way to reach your goal. Remember: when there is a will, there is a way. If your Plan "A" didn't work, create another method that will lead to your success. Remember for this law, the definition of a madman is one who does the same thing always expecting different results" -Albert Einstein-.

- ## <u>LAW 19: Don't wait for things to happen. Make it happen in its place</u>

The most successful people in life are always those who are active participants in life. Instead of waiting passively, waiting and wishing something would happen to them, people who are enterprising do not hesitate to act proactively and make things happen.

They are not those who wait for a sign of destiny or a shooting star to appear in the sky before moving. If you have a goal in sight, and you have a plan to reach it, then you will move heaven and earth to reach it.

- ## **LAW 20: Give Yourself a Reasonable Time**

Existing commitments may be a valid reason to prevent you from taking full action to achieve your goal, but you must also understand that these commitments are never going to go away. They are there for life. It is therefore unreasonable to continue to postpone the need to take a proactive stance because of your "commitments". It has to be firm with itself and give itself a deadline. Sometimes that's the only way to do things.

• <u>LAW 21: Be decisive</u>

When you commit to a plan and take action, be decisive. This will help make things smoother and make it easier for you to achieve your goal. If you are in a leadership position, it is unlikely that people will have faith in your decision if they can see that you yourself do not have faith in what you are doing. You have to show them that you know what to do and that you have the power to help everyone achieve their goals.

• <u>LAW 22 : Make a checklist</u>

Checklists show you where you are, how much progress you have made, and what still needs to be done to achieve your goal. It is an organizational and tangible list where you will put into it everything you consider necessary to achieve your goal.

• <u>LAW 23: Establish a schedule</u>

The fastest way to reach your goal is to create a calendar for it and stick to it. How many hours a day can you really set aside to reach your goal, what part of the day is the best time to reach your goal? A schedule also means having a specific place for you to do your work. Choose something that benefits the type of work you are doing and the type of person you are. Will something quiet and quiet work better for you or do you prefer to work outdoors surrounded by the sounds of nature?

• <u>LAW 24 : Make it a habit</u>

It is not enough, of course, to simply make a schedule. After all, creating one is easy, it's the part of keeping it that's difficult. To make it easier for you to keep your schedule, you have to make it a habit. Treat it as an integral part of your day that you can't miss. Your body doesn't automatically look for caffeine in the morning just because it wants to. He was trained to do so by repetitive action, strengthened by his own desire for a delicious cup of coffee. So why can't you train yourself to make your goal-achievement program part of your daily routine as well?

• <u>LAW 25 : No excuses</u>

It is possible that if you hesitate to materialize your project, start making excuses to boycott yourself and, after all, you are not going to reach any port, because you let your mind make you believe that the decision you made was the right one. But how will you know it was the right one, if you didn't take it to the real plane? That is why it is important that you carry these unbreakable laws with you throughout your life and educate your mind so that it is an ally of yours and not a machine of excuses.

- **<u>LAW 26 : If you really have to do it, then it's okay to negotiate the terms, but keep your word.</u>**

There are times when, no matter how hard I try, I can't find the energy to do the job. Or maybe you are too busy or excited about something other than your focus on achieving your goal. At times like this, there really is no choice but to "negotiate" the terms of your agenda. If you are supposed to work four hours today and can only work three, then work an extra hour tomorrow or the day after tomorrow. It is important that you specify the date for the negotiated deadline and, of course, that you keep your word.

- ## <u>LAW 27 : Eliminate distraction</u>

Distraction is the greatest enemy of your approach. Like temptation, it is insidious, you will find all kinds of ways to confuse it with your concentration. Before you begin work, you must begin by eliminating all possible sources of distraction. Distraction can also be internal. These are those doubts and concerns that do nothing to help you reach your goal. You need to practice how to identify and eliminate it so that it does not disturb your mind.

• <u>LAW 28: Meditate</u>

Numerous studies have shown that meditation techniques, like breathing exercises, are useful for clearing the mind and improving concentration. If the words and numbers you are supposed to analyze are blurred before your eyes, it is definitely time to meditate. If your anger or resentment makes it difficult for you to concentrate, meditation will also help. You don't need to chant any mantra to meditate, although if you feel it will help you, go ahead and do it. But in any case, finding a quiet place to sit down and close your eyes and let your mind deviate freely is enough.

- ## **LAW 29 : Take time off**

Sometimes, you may get a little exhausted if you've been working too hard for the past few days. When this happens, it's okay to take a short break from your work schedule. Of course, downtime can't last forever, so be sure to time it too. If you are only working for a few hours, then fifteen or thirty minutes should be enough. However, if your schedule covers the entire day, then a maximum of one hour would be sufficient.

- ## <u>LAW 30: Are you getting enough sleep?</u>

This is one of those cases where science has the last word, and according to your experts, sleep can have a significant impact on your ability to concentrate. Having enough sleep will improve your concentration. However, having too little or too much of it would cause you trouble staying focused. To get enough sleep each night, you should try to maintain a regular schedule or at least have a fixed sleep schedule. Also eliminate all sources of distraction. Consider this another goal you can focus on and take action on.

- ## **<u>Law 31: Diet matters</u>**

Diet also has to do with your ability to stay focused. An appropriate and healthy eating plan for the day will go a long way toward improving your mind's ability to work and increase endurance. Be sure to also take enough vitamins and minerals. If necessary, take health supplements.

- ## **LAW 32 : Exercise is important**

Again, you can argue that exercise may have nothing to do with helping you save money for your first car or to meet this month's sales quota, but it really does. Or at least that's what most scientific studies suggest. Like meditation, sleep, and the right one, a sufficient amount of daily exercise will also help improve the state of your mind.

• <u>LAW 33 : Enjoy what you are doing</u>

Find a way to make the process of reaching your goal enjoyable. Sometimes a change of scenery is all that is needed. Other times, you just have to find the right angle to see your situation. When you do something you like, like cooking, reading or dancing, you have no problem concentrating, do you? But if you're being forced to do something you don't quite like, then only with the most effort are you able to stay focused on your work.

- ## <u>LAW 34: How about a change of pace?</u>

The approach also depends on the rhythm. You may be trying to do things too fast or too slow for your brain to really enjoy what you're doing. When your pace is too fast, you're more likely to make mistakes. In your effort to save time, you are actually causing yourself further delays, as some of your tasks need to be redone or rectified. Using an excessively slow or relaxing pace is also not good. Don't overestimate your ability to work because that can turn into a delay if you're not careful.

• <u>LAW 35 : Consider a configuration change</u>

Sometimes, working in the same place day after day can be a bit boring, and your mind will start wandering relentlessly. When you have done everything possible to prevent your mind from wandering in vain, then a change of configuration may be necessary. Look for a different place-just for a day or two-to stay when it's time to work toward your goal. A new place may be enough to arouse your interest in them. It can also help your creativity flow and give you an idea of how best to motivate yourself.

• <u>LAW 36 : Be methodical</u>

The best way to stay focused is to be methodical. Don't pick a random spot to start working toward your goal. Whatever you're looking for. Even if it's to improve your relationship or lose weight, there will surely be a methodical or logical system to do so. Taking a methodical approach helps improve your focus because it allows you to see where you are going. If you feel a little bored concentrating on the task at hand, you can focus your attention on making the necessary adjustments to prepare for online tasks.

- ## **<u>LAW 37 : The music is 50/50</u>**

The truth is that some people find music relaxing and useful for their work. Others, however, find too relaxing to end up sleeping or too entertaining to end up forgetting the task ahead. You have to determine for yourself whether the music will serve as an aid to improve your focus or a distraction in your place.

• <u>LAW 38 : It's about what you think and feel</u>

Well-meaning friends may encourage you to try this and that to improve your concentration. Certainly, there is nothing wrong with taking his words into account. Remember, however, that each person is different. What may work for them may not work for you. That does not mean, however, that only one of you is doing the right thing. In the end, the best way to improve your approach is to do what works for you and not for others.

• <u>LAW 39 : Don't be frightened</u>

Some people will try to convince you and make you feel guilty for the time you are devoting to your goal. Whatever it is, if your goal is important to you and is not cruel or harmful to you or anyone else, then you have every right in the world to dedicate yourself to it.

- ## <u>LAW 40 : Don't let emotional conflicts get in your way.</u>

One of the worst types of distraction is emotional conflict. This type of problem consumes your concentration. If something is bothering you, resolve it immediately before returning to work. Don't let it get consumed inside you. The later you resolve these conflicts, the harder it will be to find a way to reopen the discussion.

• <u>LAW 41 : Know your priorities</u>

If you are divided between doing two things, an ultimatum must be given. What is the most important priority, the objective you are working on, or the alternative? Be brutally frank with yourself as you consider your options. If you have to choose which of the two to lose, which of them are you willing to pause or resign?

- ## **LAW 42 : Consider your energy patterns**

This may sound a little scientific, but rest assured it's not. People have different energy patterns for various reasons. Some people, for example, simply feel more energetic to work in the middle of the night because there is absolutely no distraction to worry about, with everyone sleeping soundly. Others like to work first thing in the morning because it makes them feel productive.

Their energy decreases when lunchtime arrives, but jumps again when it's early afternoon. Try to familiarize yourself with your energy pattern. Think of the days you were asked to complete a particular task.

When is it typically most efficient to complete your work? When are you less fast working on your tasks?

• <u>LAW 43 : Maximize your time</u>

Maximize your time in the sense that you must delegate what can be delegated to other capable people, allowing you to concentrate on the most critical tasks. Your approach will be ruined if you have a million things to do and are still worrying more about just three of them. If that's the case, you'll never be able to finish anything. Find people you can trust to do some of your work, and then do what you feel needs most of your attention.

- ## <u>LAW 44 : Concentrate on one side and don't look at the big picture</u>

Let's just say they gave him a whole cake to eat. Should I swallow it in one bite? It would be quite impossible to make a whole cake fit your mouth, but you can definitely eat it all, if you cut it into several slices. Sometimes focusing on the big picture alone isn't helpful. There are times when you have to first forget about the big picture and concentrate on one part of the picture at a time.

- ## **<u>LAW 45 : Be aware of errors</u>**

Nobody's perfect. There will be times when nothing you can do will be right. It's critical that you prepare ahead of time for that and take mistakes into account. If you can complete a task for thirty minutes, try to give yourself forty minutes instead. That way, you won't be terribly backed up if you end up making a mistake or two. Giving yourself concessions will also prevent your mistakes from breaking your stride.

- ## <u>LAW 46 : Practice techniques to improve memory</u>

Memory and focus are intertwined in many ways. As such, improving your memory will consequently improve your ability to concentrate. There are many ways to improve your concentration. You can find free exercises online. You can also try joining a memory training workshop or reading a memory improvement book. There are also memory training software programs you can try.

- ## **<u>LAW 47 : Learn to read effectively</u>**

Whether your goal is personal, work, or other, there will surely be a time when your goal requires you to read to nurture your mind. However, this shouldn't be a problem if you learn to read effectively. The world's fastest readers don't really read every word of the book or material they're reading. Rather, most speed readers are good at browsing and finding context clues.

Your mind and eyes are trained to find the most important parts of every page and paragraph. Even if you have limited time to finish reading something, you won't have any trouble picking up the highlights. The written word is one of the most notoriously common things that many people have difficulty concentrating on. You won't have to suffer the same fate if you just take the time to learn to read effectively.

• <u>LAW 48 : Be eager to learn</u>

No one's too smart to stop learning. It will be easier for you to concentrate on new topics or tasks if you train so that you are not reluctant to learn new things. True, old dogs have a hard time learning new tricks, but you probably have more brain cells and willpower than canines. Knowledge is a beautiful thing, and you shouldn't turn your back on the opportunity to learn something new if it is given to you.

- ## **LAW 49 : Ask and you will receive**

Religion is purely personal, as are the goals. If prayer matters a lot to you, then asking for a little divine intervention wouldn't hurt. As the Bible says, ask and you will receive. Other religions in the world are surely of the same opinion, even if they express it in different terms.

- ## <u>LAW 50 : Remember the consequences</u>

If you're extremely tempted to give up what you're doing and get lost in the fun, remember the possible consequences and that's sure to bring you back from your slip. For example, if you want to lose weight and eat that extra cup of rice tonight, it will mean having to spend an extra hour at the gym tomorrow. If you don't, it will mean that your weight will increase by two pounds. Over time, you won't be able to put on certain garments that you had in mind because you didn't have the required constancy and prioritized the successive slip rather than your discipline. Now ask yourself again, do you still want to deviate from the task before you?

- ## <u>LAW 51 : Remember that you are not the only one at stake</u>

Most of the time, the goals you want to achieve also affect others. Say that your goal is to increase benefits by 25% by the end of the year. If you don't reach your goal on time, then you won't be able to give your staff the Christmas party and year-end bonuses they so much deserve. If you don't care what consequences you will suffer from losing focus, you're probably not selfish enough to ignore how your decision will impact others.

- ## **<u>LAW 52 : Divert all calls to your voicemail</u>**

Phones of all kinds are also a source of distraction. Change the message on your answering machine so people know you can't afford to be disturbed. If they really care about you, they're sure to understand. Be sure, however, to let them know that you will be checking your mailbox every hour. If they have a drastic need to contact you, then they'd better start typing in their emails or keywords in the what app.

- ## <u>LAW 53: Limit your email check or whats app to five minutes per hour.</u>

It really can't be any more than that because you're only supposed to respond to emails or what's apps that absolutely require a response. Anything that is not important should be put aside. You have to be very firm about this rule or you will end up postponing it again.

- ## <u>LAW 54 : Do you remember that list? Don't forget to check it</u>

Seeing your checklist near completion will always work as a great stimulus to your confidence. If you were able to accomplish so much already, you can surely accomplish the rest of your tasks.

• <u>Law 55: Use affirmations</u>

Affirmations are basically positive affirmations that tell yourself repeatedly like a mantra. This is supposed to help you enjoy a positive mood and have more confidence to achieve your goal. Some people say that statements should not use potential forms of verbs such as "I can. To further convince yourself of your abilities, affirmations should begin with words like "I want..." and "I am..." because they demonstrate more self-confidence and self-confidence.

- ## **<u>LAW 56 : Think of internal rewards to congratulate yourself</u>**

Positive reinforcement is always a good thing, so don't forget to pat yourself on the back when you've completed one of the most fundamental steps in achieving your goal. Now is the time to start tweeting about your last task. Let yourself be carried away by the compliments of your loved ones and friends, as this will surely set you in motion.

• <u>LAW 57: Reward yourself materially too</u>

Material rewards certainly matter too. There is nothing extravagant about it although if it is something you can afford and really want, then you can also promise yourself a great reward when you reach your goal. Try to be a little creative about your rewards. You can pamper yourself with a massage, take a trip out of town, or indulge in a dinner night at the most expensive restaurant in the area. It can also be something as simple as letting the weekend go by without doing anything and enjoying other small luxuries for which you normally don't have time. Just think about what will make you happy and do it.

• <u>LAW 58 : Re-evaluate your goal</u>

Sometimes the reason you have trouble motivating yourself is because your goal is no longer important. From time to time, you should re-evaluate your goal and find out if it is still as important or if it needs a little redefinition.

- ## <u>LAW 59 : Always look on the bright side</u>

Don't think there's no good side, because there always is. If you feel that you have bottomed out, there is still a positive side. When you are down, there is no other way but to rise up and continue on your way.

• <u>LAW 60 : Look for a role model to follow</u>

A role model doesn't have to be perfect, famous or even older than you. Rather, that role model has qualities that you both admire and want to have because you will become a better person for it. When you feel like giving up, think of your role model. No one is immune to temptations, but each person has the power to say no to them. Your role model was strong enough to say no to distraction and stay focused. Surely you can too. In the end, they are both mortal, flesh and blood. You are capable of doing the same, as long as you put your mind to it.

• <u>LAW 61 : Seeking Inspiration</u>

The role models are different from inspiration. The role models are someone you try to emulate. However, people, things or places to be inspired are also like goals. Why is your goal to get rich? It's because you want to give your parents the opportunity to retire early. Well, then your parents are your inspiration. When you're extremely frustrated by what's going on and feel like throwing in the towel, imagine your parents going back to their path.

• <u>LAW 62 : Don't stop harnessing the power of visualization</u>

It is easier to stay motivated when you are able to visualize the achievement of your dream. Close your eyes and try to imagine what would happen if you reached your goal. How would you feel? What would happen next? Make it so vivid that you can feel the joy of reaching your dream.

• <u>LAW 63 : Proverbs are there for a reason</u>

Ancient proverbs and sayings are used in different spheres of life. That is because they are true. Clichés have become clichés because they have been said too often and are essentially facts. If there are no words you can personally think of to motivate yourself, do not hesitate to resort to the power of proverbs.

• <u>LAW 64: Carpe Diem!</u>

In Latin it means "ENJOY THE MOMENT". Tell yourself that the opportunity your goal represents only comes once in a lifetime. If you do not seize the day, or the moment, then that opportunity may not come up again. Are you willing to take that risk?

- ## **<u>Law 65: Think of the last time you worked against all odds and won.</u>**

You are a powerful person; however, sometimes you may need to be reminded. If your confidence has plummeted for any reason, remember the last time you worked against all odds. Think of the time when no one had your back and only you had faith in yourself. You did it then once, you can do it again. Just believe in yourself.

• <u>LAW 66 : Participate in motivational seminars from time to time</u>

If you've never tried to attend a motivational seminar, it's easy for you to say that these so-called self-help gurus are just trying to con you out of your money. If you have no idea which of today's many inspirational speakers is the best, don't hesitate to ask for recommendations. Check on the Internet for revisions as well.

- ## **LAW 67 : Remember the little things**

Motivation is also a matter of point of view. If you are tired of working or doing something for the sake of reaching your goal alone, then do it only for the sake of your goal. Do it because you love it and it makes you feel good. Sometimes the journey counts more than the actual destination.

• <u>LAW 68 : Keep a Gratitude Diary</u>

If Oprah itself does this, then surely everyone has the propensity to benefit from it as well. For every day, try to think of as many things as you can for which you are sincerely grateful. If you feel you have absolutely nothing to be grateful for, then you are wrong. You're alive, aren't you? You can still read this and then that already gives you three reasons to be grateful. Remember: motivation is a matter of perspective. If you can't see it from one angle, then you could probably see it from another.

- ## <u>LAW 69: Are you tempted to give up?</u>

When you feel that you have reached the end of your chain, make one last big push by doing 5 more. Or if you're one step away from giving in to tiredness or sleep, do just 3 or even one more. You may not have completed your schedule today, but knowing that you've done your best is enough to give you an energetic and motivated attitude for the next day.

• <u>LAW 70 : Failure is not an option</u>

It's true he's not stuck on the moon, flying on Apollo 11, but does it really matter? You just have to imagine yourself in the same scenario back against the wall and that's sure to be enough motivation to work hard. Previously, you've learned how to overcome failures and the importance of not punishing yourself for it. Still, that doesn't mean you can get away with it, without having to worry about it.

- ## **<u>Law 71: Never say never</u>**

You can change tactics, rest for a while and redefine your goal, but none of that means you're quitting. It should never be part of your vocabulary. Even if that sounds contradictory; the moment you start to have doubts that are the moment you start to lose.

• <u>LAW 72 : Aim to be better every day</u>

Aim to improve yourself and your situation. Having the enthusiasm to take each day as learning and as a perfection of your being, will help you to be open to new emotions, feelings, experiences. It will take you out of the fateful routine and make you feel renewed every day.

- ## **LAW 73 : Expect the best but be prepared for the worst**

Motivation can be a double-edged sword. On the one hand, it can go through the clouds of depression and doubt, especially when your motivation is worthwhile and you're successful in what you're trying to achieve, but what if you don't get what you want? Motivation can end up hurting you as you prepare for a fall. This will happen if you haven't prepared for the worst either. Preparing for the bad means that you have at least considered the possibility and taken the necessary steps to deal with it.

- ## <u>LAW 74 : Do it no matter how long it takes</u>

It is very important that you do not abandon your goal just because your path to success turned out to be longer and more twisted than expected. That is the card that life has given you, so take care of it and move on again.

- ## **<u>LAW 75: Don't let any source of frustration, problems, or depression get worse. Eliminate it immediately.</u>**

If something worries you and makes it hard to keep you focused and motivated, get rid of it right away. Cut it out and don't wait for it to turn into a total disaster.

• <u>LAW 76 : Think of all those who didn't get as far as you did.</u>

Sometimes, a person has a tendency to keep comparing himself to those who feel that he is better than he who doesn't realize how much he himself has done. When you realize that, you will feel in harmony with your being, but always keep in mind that this does not make you better than others. Motivation is a matter of time. You will achieve your goal just have to work hard and keep your eyes on your goal.

<u>CONCLUSION</u>

At the end of the day, there is a thought that you must remember when you are contemplating your next step: The only difference between a successful man and a failed man is that one of them stopped trying.